Oxford Progressive English Readers provide a wide range of enjoyable reading at six language levels. Text lengths range from 8,000 words at the Starter level, to about 35,000 words at Level 5. The latest methods of text analysis, using specially designed software, ensure that readability is carefully controlled.

The aim of the series is to present stories to engage the interest of the reader; to intrigue, mystify, amuse, delight and stimulate the imagination.

MERRY CHRISTMAS

A
CHRISTMAS
CAROL
Charles Dickens
OXFORD
UNIVERSITY PRESS

OXFORD
UNIVERSITY PRESS

Oxford University Press is a department of the University of Oxford. It furthers the University's objective of excellence in research, scholarship, and education by publishing worldwide. Oxford is a registered trade mark of Oxford University Press in the UK and in certain other countries

Published in Hong Kong by
Oxford University Press (China) Limited
18th Floor, Warwick House East, Taikoo Place, 979 King's Road, Quarry Bay, Hong Kong

First Edition published in 1992
Second Edition published in 2005

ISBN: 978-0-19-597134-7

15 17 19 20 18 16

Acknowledgements:
Illustrated by Choy Man Yung
Syllabus design and text analysis by David Foulds

Contents

Introduction

A Christmas Carol is the first of five 'Christmas Books' published during the Christmas season in Victorian England. It is seen as a celebration of Christmas.

At the beginning of Queen Victoria's reign, the celebration of Christmas was in decline. The Industrial Revolution meant that workers had little time to celebrate Christmas. The Queen's husband, Prince Albert, brought the German custom of decorating a Christmas tree to England. The singing of Christmas carols became popular, and the first Christmas card appeared in the 1840s. But it was the Christmas stories of Charles Dickens, particularly *A Christmas Carol,* that made people want to celebrate and enjoy Christmas. With *A Christmas Carol*, Dickens gave Christmas a new status. Many tried to celebrate Christmas in the same way as in the story.

When people think of Dickens, they think of Christmas. There is a story that when Dickens died in 1870, a little girl asked, 'Mr Dickens dead? Then will Father Christmas die too?'

A Christmas Carol tells the story of Christmas in England, but how is Christmas celebrated in other countries? In Australia, Christmas comes in the middle of summer. Instead of a dinner of roast goose in snowy winter, Australians might be celebrating their Christmas on the beach, with a barbecue and salad! In Spain, Christmas Eve is the time for a big family dinner. Instead of Christmas Day, the big celebration is on 6 January. This is the twelfth night after Christmas or 'The Festival of the Three Kings'. It celebrates the time when the three wise men or kings brought gifts to the baby Jesus. The Spanish open their presents on this day.

About Charles Dickens

Charles Dickens was born in 1812 in Portsmouth, England. He enjoyed a happy early childhood until his family moved to London in 1823, and the family didn't have much money. At the age of twelve, he had to work with other child workers pasting labels on bottles of shoe polish in a factory. This experience had a great effect on him and can be seen in his work. Dickens was always concerned for the suffering of the poor and the disadvantaged.

Dickens worked as a lawyer's clerk and a journalist before he became famous as the greatest English novelist of the Victorian era. Besides *A Christmas Carol*, his best-loved works include *Oliver Twist*, *David Copperfield, Bleak House, A Tale of Two Cities, Great Expectations,* and *Our Mutual Friend.*

1
Scrooge of 'Scrooge and Marley'

When our story begins, Jacob Marley was dead. He had been dead for a long time. Of course Scrooge knew he was dead. Scrooge had worked with Marley for many years, and Scrooge was his only friend. Marley's death was sad, but Scrooge was not unhappy for long. On the day of Marley's funeral, Scrooge was working hard in his office.

SCROOGE AND MARLEY was painted on the front door of Scrooge's office. That was the name of the business.

Although Marley had died years ago, Scrooge never painted out Marley's name. People who did not know Scrooge sometimes called him 'Scrooge', and sometimes they called him 'Marley'. Scrooge answered to both names. It was all the same to him.

Scrooge never gave away any money. He never told anyone anything. He was as secret as a fish. He had a cold heart and an unkind face, a pointed nose, red eyes and thin blue lips. When he was young he had had dark hair, but now it was all white. People said there was snow on his head and over his eyes and on his mouth. He carried bad weather about with him.

Nobody ever came to him in the street, saying with a happy face, 'My dear Ebenezer' (that was Scrooge's first name), 'how are you? When will you come to my home to see my wife and me?' No beggar ever asked him for money. No children ever asked him what time it was. No man or woman ever asked Scrooge the way to any place. Even the dogs seemed afraid of him.

When they saw him coming they would pull their owners out of the way until he had passed. But do you think Scrooge cared? Not at all. He was very pleased that no one troubled him!

Scrooge's nephew visits him

One afternoon, on the day before Christmas, which is the best day of all the days in the year, old Scrooge sat busy in his office. It was cold, dark, December weather. Outside, the people in the street were walking up and down. They stamped their feet on the road to keep themselves warm. It was just after three o'clock, but quite dark. Since morning the sun had been covered with thick clouds. There had been very little light all day.

The door of Scrooge's office was open. He was watching his clerk in the next room. In Scrooge's room there was a small fire. The fire in the clerk's room was even smaller. It seemed to be just one piece of coal. The clerk had put a long, old piece of cloth — his scarf — around his neck to keep himself warm.

'A Happy Christmas, Uncle, God bless you!' someone said.

Scrooge jumped up in surprise.

It was the voice of Scrooge's nephew. The young man had come into the office so quickly that Scrooge had not known he was there.

'Bah! Humbug!' said Scrooge. 'Humbug!' was a word Scrooge loved to use about anything he thought stupid or foolish. 'Go away! Go away!'

Scrooge's nephew was quite warm from walking quickly in the December cold. His face was red and good to look at. His eyes shone with happiness.

'Are you telling me to go away at Christmas, Uncle?' said Scrooge's nephew. 'You don't mean that, I'm sure.'

'I do,' said Scrooge. 'Bah to your Happy Christmas! Why are *you* happy? You're too poor to be happy.'

'Why are you *unhappy*?' said the nephew, laughing. 'You're too rich to be unhappy!'

Scrooge said 'Bah!' and 'Humbug!' again, and 'Go away'. He could not think of anything better to say.

'Don't be angry, Uncle,' the nephew said.

'What else can I be,' replied his uncle, 'when I live in this world of foolish people? Happy Christmas! Bah to a Happy Christmas! What does Christmas mean to you? It is just a time for buying things when you do not have the money to pay for them. It is just a time when you find yourself a year older but not an hour richer.'

Scrooge went on, 'A man who goes about saying "A Happy Christmas" is a fool. Someone should take him away and cook him in his own Christmas pudding! That's what I think of "A Happy Christmas!"'

'Uncle!' cried the nephew.

'Nephew!' replied the uncle. 'You go away and enjoy Christmas in your way, and leave me to enjoy Christmas in my way.'

'Enjoy it, Uncle?' repeated Scrooge's nephew. 'But you don't enjoy it.'

'Then let me enjoy not enjoying it,' said Scrooge. 'It has never done you much good!'

The nephew said, 'I know there are many things from which I have not earned money. Christmas is one of these things. But I have always thought of Christmas as a time to love, forgive and be kind. Christmas is a good and pleasant time. It is a time when men and women are happy to think of others as their friends through life, and not as strangers. And therefore, Uncle, though Christmas has never put a piece of money into my pocket, I believe that it has done me much good. And I say, "God Bless Christmas".'

The clerk in the small office in the next room called out happily, 'Yes, quite right, sir, God Bless Christmas!' He was the only clerk who worked for Scrooge. His name was Bob Cratchit.

Cratchit saw Scrooge looking at him. He went to the fire and turned the small piece of coal over, but that stopped it burning. His cold little room became even colder.

'Let me hear another word from you,' said Scrooge to the clerk, 'and you'll enjoy your Christmas Day looking for a new job.' He turned to his nephew. 'The way you talk is quite clever, sir. You should become a politician.'

'Don't be angry, Uncle. Come and have dinner with us tomorrow.'

Scrooge said that he would never do that.

'But why?' cried Scrooge's nephew. 'Why?'

'Why did you get married?' said Scrooge.

'Because I fell in love.'

'Because you fell in love!' repeated Scrooge. He thought love was the one thing more foolish than 'A Happy Christmas'. 'Now, I am very busy, so please leave me to do my work. Good afternoon!'

'I am really sorry that you will not think about it. There is nothing to stop us from being friends. I came to you because it was Christmas. I'll always come to see you and ask you to be happy with us at Christmas time. So, a Happy Christmas, Uncle.'

'Good afternoon!'

'And a Happy New Year!'

'Good afternoon!'

'And God Bless You, dear Uncle!'

'Good afternoon!'

His nephew left the room smiling. He went to Bob Cratchit to wish him a Happy Christmas. Though the clerk was cold, his heart was warmer than Scrooge's.

Scrooge listened to them talking. He thought, 'I pay my clerk less than one pound a week. With that he has to look after a wife and children. How can he talk about a Happy Christmas. I believe the world is going mad.'

2
The Office is Closed for Christmas

When Bob Cratchit let Scrooge's nephew out, two other people came in. They were big gentlemen. They both looked kind-hearted, and they both had happy faces. They now stood, with their hats off, in Scrooge's office. They held books and papers in their hands. They were collecting money for the poor. They bowed to Scrooge.

'*Scrooge and Marley,* I believe,' said one of the gentlemen, looking at his papers. 'Am I speaking to Mr Scrooge or Mr Marley?'

'Mr Marley has been dead for seven years,' Scrooge replied. 'He died seven years ago on this very night.'

'We are sure that you are just as kind as dear Mr Marley was,' said the gentleman, handing some papers to Scrooge.

Scrooge certainly was just as kind as Marley. Marley never gave any money to anyone. In that way the two men were equal.

'At this time of the year,' said the gentleman, 'we should all try to help the poor.' He took out a pencil and a small book. He hoped to write down how much Scrooge would give. 'There are many poor people in London these days,' he continued. 'Many thousands of people are in need of the simplest things, even food and clothes.'

'Aren't there any prisons?' asked Scrooge.

'There are plenty of prisons,' said the gentleman, surprised. He put down his pencil.

'And poorhouses — there are still plenty of those, are there not?'

'There are, but I wish I could say there were not. They are cruel places!'

'I was afraid, from what you were saying, that someone had closed them! I am very glad to hear that they are still there,' said Scrooge, and he smiled.

Scrooge will give nothing

The two gentlemen looked at each other as if they were not sure they could believe their ears. Did Scrooge really mean what he had said?

'Well, the poorhouses do not give any help at all to the great numbers of poor people outside them,' the gentleman continued. 'We are trying to get some money to buy meat and drink and winter clothes for these people. We chose this time of the year because it is the time when poor people feel most unhappy. What shall I write down for you, Mr Scrooge?'

'Nothing.'

'Perhaps you mean that you do not wish your name to be written down in our book?'

'I mean that I do not wish to give any money. I wish to be left alone,' said Scrooge. 'You ask me what I wish, gentlemen, and that is my answer. I do not spend money making myself happy at Christmas, and I have no money to make other people happy. I pay taxes. The tax money is used to help the prisons and the poorhouses, and that costs me enough. Those poor people you speak of can go there!'

'Many can't go there, and many think it would be better to die than go there.'

'If they think it would be better to die, then that is what they must do. The numbers of the poor will grow less. But, excuse me for saying this, I don't really know that they would wish to die. What you say may not be true.'

'You should believe it.'

'It's not my business,' Scrooge replied. 'It's enough for a man to understand his own business, and not to worry about other people's. I always have plenty to do just looking after mine. Good afternoon, gentlemen!'

The gentlemen saw that it would be useless to say anything more, and they went away. Scrooge went back to his work. He felt very pleased and much happier than he had been all that day.

Scrooge closes his office for Christmas

It grew darker and colder. Both outside and in, the air was so cold it felt as if it were biting you.

A child sang a Christmas carol outside the front door of Scrooge's office. Scrooge picked up a ruler, went to the front door and opened it so quickly that the small singer ran away in fear. Once more it was quiet. The only sound you could hear was the sad sound of the cold wind blowing under the office door.

At last it was time to stop work. Scrooge angrily climbed out of his chair. He told Bob Cratchit that he could go. He put on his hat.

'You want to be at home all tomorrow, I believe?' said Scrooge.

'If it is all right, sir.'

'It's not all right. If I take some money from you for staying at home all day you will think I am a very unkind person, I'm quite sure.'

The clerk smiled.

'And yet,' said Scrooge, 'you don't see that when I pay you a day's money for doing no work, then that is bad for me.'

The clerk said that it was only once a year.

'That's a poor excuse for taking a man's money every twenty-fifth of December,' said Scrooge. He pulled his coat well round his neck. 'All right, then, you may have the whole day. But make sure you come here much earlier the next morning.'

The clerk promised that he would, and Scrooge walked out.

In a second, Bob Cratchit closed the office and went out, too. The ends of his scarf hung below his waist, for he had no coat. He slid down the ice in the road, at the end of a line of boys. Then he went back and did it again. He did it twenty times because very soon it would be Christmas Day, the best day of all the days of the year. Then he ran home to his small house in Camden Town as fast as he could, to play Christmas games with his children.

3
Scrooge Meets an Old Friend

Scrooge ate his dinner alone in his usual restaurant. First he read all the newspapers, and then he amused himself by reading his bank book. After that he left the restaurant and went home to go to bed.

He lived in some dark rooms, in a dark building, up many dark stairs. Once his friend Marley had lived there, too. Now only Scrooge lived there. All the other rooms in the building were used as offices during the day. At night there was no one else in the whole building. Scrooge was quite alone. That is why he liked living there!

He knew every stone on the path of that black place, but it was so dark he had to feel his way with his hand until he reached his door.

The face on the door knocker

There was a big, metal door knocker on Scrooge's door. There was nothing at all strange about it. It was, perhaps, larger than most door knockers, but that was all. Scrooge had seen it every night and every morning during the time that he had lived in the place.

When Scrooge looked at something, he always knew exactly what it was. He never thought it might be something else. So it is very hard to explain what happened next.

Scrooge put the key in the lock of the door. As he started to turn the key he looked at the door knocker. He saw, not a knocker, but Marley's face!

Marley's face! It was not as dark as the doorway around it. It was lit with a strange, pale light. It was not angry or fierce. It looked at Scrooge sadly, just as Marley used to look. Its glasses were pushed up into its hair. Marley used to do just the same thing.

Marley's hair was moving. It moved as if there was a soft wind blowing very gently, or hot air rising from below. The eyes were wide open, but they were still. They looked straight at Scrooge. That, and the strange light, made Marley's face a frightening sight.

Scrooge could not move, he was so afraid. Then, as his eyes took a second, closer look at the face, it changed into a knocker again.

Scrooge was very surprised. In fact, he had gone cold with fright. He turned the key quickly, opened the door and walked in. First he lit his lamp, and then in less then a second he went back to the door. He looked carefully at it, first at the front and then at the back. But the only thing on the front of the door was the door knocker, and at the back of the door there was nothing at all. 'Humbug!' said Scrooge, and he closed the door with a bang.

The strange carriage

The noise sounded through the house like thunder. Every room above, and every room below, made its own special sound. But Scrooge was not afraid of noises. He locked the door and walked across the hall. He went up the stairs slowly, holding his small lamp high.

The stairs in Scrooge's house were very wide. If you had seen them you would have said they were wide enough to drive a carriage up. And that is what Scrooge thought he saw.

As he slowly climbed the stairs, his lamp, which was just one small lamp in a large, dark place, made strange shadows. Scrooge thought he could see a carriage moving slowly along in front of him. He was walking at the same speed, behind it. It was a hearse, a special carriage used at funerals to take dead bodies to be buried in the cemetery. He did not know whose funeral it was. He did not care. Scrooge was not easily frightened by shadows!

He went into his room, closed his door and locked himself in. In this way he felt quite safe. He took off his winter coat, his jacket, his collar and tie. He put on his night clothes. He put slippers on his feet, and a night cap on his head. Then he sat down at the side of his fire to take his usual evening drink.

Strange noises

As Scrooge rested his head on the back of his chair, his eyes looked towards a bell that hung by the door. The bell was never used and nobody remembered why it was there.

As he looked at the bell, it began to move. Scrooge, frightened, sat up straight. The bell moved so softly at first that it did not make a sound. Soon, however, it started ringing, louder and louder. Then every other bell in the house started ringing at the same time.

This lasted perhaps half a minute, or a minute, but it seemed like an hour. Then, suddenly, all the bells stopped. They were followed by a noise deep down below in the dark old building. It sounded as if someone was dragging something very heavy across the floor. You could hear the noise of small pieces of metal hitting against other pieces of metal. Was it a chain? Was someone dragging a heavy chain across the floor? Then Scrooge thought about ghosts. People say that in some houses ghosts pull chains along with them.

'Bah! Humbug!' said Scrooge. Then there was a great noise, and he heard a door below break open. He heard the chains, much louder. Someone, or something, was coming up the stairs, straight towards his door.

'This is just some nonsense,' said Scrooge. 'I don't believe it. I won't believe it.' But it was not long before he had second thoughts about that. Without stopping, a large, strange-looking thing came through the thick, heavy doors of Scrooge's room. It passed straight into the room in front of his eyes. As soon as it came in, the flames in the fire jumped up. From them a voice cried out, 'I know him! That is the ghost of Jacob Marley,' and the flames died down again.

The same face, the very same face! Marley in his usual clothes and boots! There was the chain, fastened around his waist. It was long and lay about him on the floor like a great tail. Scrooge looked at it very carefully. Fixed to the chain were keys, bank books, money boxes, and other heavy things.

4

Scrooge Talks to Marley's Ghost

Scrooge looked at the ghost again. He could see right through him. He could see the two buttons on the back of the ghost's coat, behind him.

'What now?' said Scrooge, as hard and cold as ever. 'What do you want with me?'

'Much,' said Marley's voice.

'Who are you?'

'Ask me who I *was*.'

'Who *were* you, then?' said Scrooge, speaking louder.

'In life, I was your friend, Jacob Marley.'

'Will you — can you sit down?' said Scrooge, who was not sure about the things that ghosts could do.

'I can.'

'Do it, then.'

Scrooge did not know whether a ghost, which he could see through, would be able to sit in a chair. But the ghost did. It sat down at the side of the fire, facing Scrooge.

'You don't believe in me?' asked the Ghost.

'I don't,' said Scrooge.

'You can see and hear me, but you won't believe in me. Why are you afraid of your own thoughts?'

'Because a little thing can easily change my thoughts and make them strange. Perhaps you are just some food I have eaten which has made me ill. You may be a piece of bad fish, or perhaps some half-cooked meat, or a bit of cake that has been lying about for too long!'

Scrooge did not usually make jokes. Certainly he did not feel very happy then. He talked like that in order to try to forget the cold fear inside him. The voice of the Ghost had frightened him until he shook with fear.

'You see this button?' said Scrooge. He tried to make the eyes of the Ghost look away. He did not like the Ghost looking at him.

'I do,' replied the Ghost.

'But you are not looking at it.'

'But I see it.'

'Well,' went on Scrooge, 'if I eat this, it will make me ill. I will start seeing things that are not there. I will probably see ghosts following me about for days.'

The Ghost did not look pleased.

'I can make ghosts come,' continued Scrooge, 'and I can make them go. I do not wish to see you. So go away, I say.'

'You are making your own chain'

At this, the Ghost jumped up from the chair, gave a great, frightening cry, and shook its chain with a noise that filled Scrooge's heart with fear. Scrooge held on to his chair tightly to keep himself from falling, but his fear of the ghost was too much. At last, he fell to his knees. 'Oh Ghost,' he said, 'why do you trouble me?'

'Do you believe in me or do you not?'

'I do,' said Scrooge, 'Oh yes, I do, I do. I must.'

The Ghost sat down.

'But tell me,' said Scrooge, 'why is a ghost walking about on the earth? Why have you come here, to trouble me?'

'In his life every person must walk among other people, and travel far and wide. If a person does not do this, his ghost must do it after he has died. It then travels round the world. It must look at things it cannot enjoy — things which other people can have on earth and which make them happy.'

'Why are you wearing that chain?' asked Scrooge.

'I wear the chain I made for myself when I was alive. It is the chain of not-caring. It is the chain of self-love. It is the chain that comes when you think making money is more important than caring about other people. When I was alive I did not know what I was doing. I made this chain piece by piece. I made it cheerfully, and I wore it cheerfully. Does its metal seem strange to you?'

Scrooge shook with fear more and more.

'I can tell you this,' the Ghost continued. 'You, too, are making a chain for yourself. Seven years ago your chain was as long and as heavy as mine is now. Since then you have made it much longer and much heavier.' Scrooge looked on the floor behind him. He was afraid he would see his chain there, but he saw nothing.

'Jacob,' he asked, 'tell me more. Please help me.'

'I cannot help you,' the Ghost replied, 'and I cannot tell you everything I would like to. I am only allowed a little more time. I cannot stay; I cannot rest anywhere. When I was alive I never left our little money-making office. Now, I have to travel many, many long miles.'

'You travel very slowly, then?' asked Scrooge in a quiet businesslike way.

'Slowly!'

'Seven years dead, and travelling all the time?'

'Yes, I have been travelling the whole time. No rest, no peace,' and the ghost cried out, a great loud, sad cry. It lifted up a part of its chain, then threw it to the ground again. 'At this time of the year I am saddest. When I was alive, why did I walk past so many other people with my eyes turned down? Why didn't I look up into the sky and see God's star, the same star which led three kings to a poor home where a little child lay sleeping? Was I afraid because I knew its light would lead me into the homes of the poor?'

Scrooge was not at all happy to hear the ghost talking like this.

'Hear me,' cried the Ghost, 'my time is nearly gone.'

'I will,' said Scrooge, 'but don't punish me so much, Jacob.'

'I cannot tell you how I am able to come to you in this shape. But I can tell you that I have often sat by your side like this, and you have not seen me.'

That was not a pleasant thought for Scrooge.

Scrooge is given some help

'I am here tonight to tell you that you do not need to become like me,' continued the Ghost. 'I can help you that much, Ebenezer.'

'You were always a good friend to me,' said Scrooge, 'thank you, Jacob.'

'Three ghosts will visit you.' Scrooge's face showed that he was afraid when he heard this.

'Is that the help you are talking about, Jacob?' he asked in a weak voice.

'It is.'

'I think I don't want to be helped, then,' said Scrooge.

'If they don't visit you, you will certainly become like me. Expect the first ghost tomorrow when you hear the clock strike one.'

'Couldn't I see them all at the same time,' asked Scrooge, 'and get it done quickly?'

'Expect the second ghost on the second night at one o'clock. The third ghost will come on the next night at exactly twelve o'clock. You will see me no more. For your own good, remember what I have told you.'

When the Ghost had said these words, it stood up and walked to the window. The window began to open slowly as the Ghost moved towards it. At each step it opened a little more. By the time the ghost reached it, it was wide open.

Scrooge followed and looked out. He saw that the night air was full of ghosts, all of them wearing long, heavy chains. When Marley's ghost joined them, they flew away, quickly. The dark, cold winter sky became still and empty.

For a while, Scrooge stood at the window, thinking about what he had seen and heard. Then he shut the window quickly.

'Bah!' he said to himself. 'Hum—,' he said. He was going to say 'Humbug!' but stopped. It had been a strange day and Scrooge was not quite so sure of himself as usual. He went to bed.

5
The Ghost of Christmas Past

Scrooge woke up. It was very dark. He looked around his room. He could just see where the window was, but even that was almost as dark as everything else. Then he heard the bell of a nearby church clock strike twelve. He was surprised, for it had been two o'clock when he went to bed. He thought that the clock was wrong.

'It can't be true!' he said. 'Have I slept through a whole day, and far into another night? Or is it twelve o'clock in the middle of the day and something has happened to the sun. It cannot be possible!'

Then he suddenly remembered Marley's words. 'Expect the first ghost tomorrow when the clock strikes one,' Marley had said. He decided to stay awake until the hour had passed. Also, now that he had remembered about the ghost, he was too frightened to go back to sleep.

At one o'clock the bell of the church clock sounded a deep, slow, *one*. At once, a bright light appeared in the room. In a second, Scrooge found himself face to face with someone from another world.

It looked very strange, like a child but also like an old man. Its long hair was white like an old man's hair, but the face was young. Its skin was pale, but beautiful. The arms and hands were long and very strong. Its legs, like its arms, had nothing on them. It wore a white coat, and a beautiful shining belt around its waist. Although it held some dark green holly leaves in its hand,

its coat was covered with summer flowers. The strangest thing of all was the bright, clear light coming from its head. It held, under its arm, a long, pointed cap which, when placed on the head, would hide the light.

'Are you the ghost I was told to expect?' said Scrooge.

'I am.'

The voice was soft and gentle, but it seemed to come from a distance instead of close to him.

'Who and what are you?' Scrooge asked.

'I am the Ghost of Christmas Past.'

'Long past?' asked Scrooge.

'No, your past. Your past life.'

Scrooge suddenly had a strong wish. He did not know why, but he wanted to see the Ghost wearing the cap. He asked him to put it on.

'What!' cried the Ghost. 'Do you want me to put out the light I give so soon? Is it not enough that you are the one who made this cap? Is it not enough that, because of you, I must carry it with me all the time?'

Scrooge said that he did not mean to hurt anyone. He did not know that he had made a cap for any ghost. He was then brave enough to ask why the Ghost had come.

'Because you need my help,' said the Ghost. Scrooge thanked him very much, but thought that a good night's sleep was all the help he wanted. The Ghost heard his thoughts, for it said at once, 'Take care!' and with its strong hand held him gently by the arm.

'Rise and walk with me,' said the Ghost.

Its hand, though gentle as a woman's, would not leave him. Scrooge rose into the air. He found that the Ghost was going to the window. He held its coat and pulled back, trying to stop it.

'I shall fall,' he said.

The Ghost put its hand on Scrooge's heart, saying, 'I shall hold you up.'

As the words were spoken, they passed through the wall.

Scrooge goes back in time

Suddenly, there was light all around them. They stood upon an open road, with fields on either side.

They could not see London. They were far away from the town, outside in the country. It was a cold, clear, winter day with snow on the ground.

'I can't believe it!' said Scrooge as he looked around him. 'I used to live in this place. I was a boy here.'

The Ghost watched him.

'Your lip is shaking,' said the ghost, 'and what is that upon your face? Are you crying?'

Scrooge answered roughly that it was nothing at all. 'Just lead me anywhere you wish,' he said.

'Why do you want me to lead you. Don't you remember the way?'

'Remember it!' cried Scrooge. 'I can find my way with my eyes shut.'

'It is strange that you have not thought about this place for so many years,' said the Ghost. 'Let us go on.'

They walked along the road. Scrooge knew every garden and post and tree. Then they came to a little town with a bridge and a church, and a small river. Some boys, riding horses, came towards them. They were calling to other boys. They were all enjoying themselves. It seemed as if the fields were full of lovely music. Even the air laughed happily when it heard the boys calling.

The boys walked on and, as they reached him, Scrooge could not believe his eyes. He knew these boys. He could name every one of them. They were his old friends. They were the boys he had grown up with.

Why was he so glad to see them? Why did his cold eyes shine, and his heart beat quickly as they went past? Why was he filled with joy when they wished each other a Happy Christmas, and left to go to their different homes? What was a Happy Christmas to Scrooge? Had he ever enjoyed Christmas?

Scrooge sees himself as a child

'The school is not quite empty,' said the Ghost. 'A boy, all alone and forgotten by his friends, is still there.'

Scrooge said he knew it, and tears began to fall down his old face.

They left the high road, and walked along a path that Scrooge knew well. Soon they reached a building made of dark red brick. It was a large building, but it had not been well cared for. The walls were wet, the windows broken and the doors left wide open. The rooms were big and cold. Everywhere was covered with dirt and dust. Everywhere the tables and chairs were old and broken.

The Ghost and Scrooge went across the hall to a door at the back of the house. It opened before them, and they went into a long, ugly room, with lines of desks in it. Scrooge sat down and tried to remember himself as he used to be.

He knew every sound in the room, and every movement from the tree outside. These all touched his heart. Scrooge's tears fell more and more.

The Ghost touched him on the arm, and pointed to a young boy, reading quietly.

'Is that …' said Scrooge. 'Is that really me?'

'It was,' said the Ghost.

'I wish,' Scrooge began, putting his hand into his pocket and looking about him, '… but it is too late now!'

'What is the matter?' asked the Ghost.

'Nothing,' said Scrooge, 'nothing. There was a boy singing a Christmas carol at my door last night. I am sorry that I did not give him something; that is all.'

The Ghost smiled kindly and said, 'Let's see another Christmas in your past life.'

The young boy grew larger at these words. The room became a little darker and dirtier. Scrooge did not know how this happened. He only knew that what he was seeing was quite right. Everything had been just like that.

There he was, alone again, when all the other boys had gone home for their holidays. He was not reading now, but walking up and down sadly. The door opened. A little girl ran in and put her arms round his neck, saying, 'Dear brother, I have come to bring you home.'

'Home, little sister?'

'Yes,' said the child, 'home for ever. Father is much kinder now, and home is happy. He sent me to bring you. You will never come back here.' She began to pull him to the door as hard as she could.

'She was never very strong,' said the ghost, 'but she had a kind heart, didn't she?'

'Yes, she was always so kind.'

'You liked her a lot, I believe.'

'Yes.'

'She is dead now. But she had children, didn't she?'

'One child,' Scrooge said.

'True,' said the Ghost. 'Your nephew.'

Scrooge said nothing for a few seconds. Then he answered, 'That's right. My nephew.'

6
Scrooge at Fezziwig's

Everything changed. Now they were in the busy streets of London, although it seemed as if they had only just left the school. The Ghost stopped outside one of the offices, and asked Scrooge if he knew it.

'Know it?' said Scrooge. 'I learnt my business here.'

They went in. Scrooge saw an old gentleman sitting behind a tall desk. 'Why, it's old Fezziwig, alive again,' he cried.

Old Fezziwig put down his pen and looked at the clock. It was seven o'clock. He rubbed his hands together and laughed. In a happy voice, he called out, 'Hello there, Ebenezer, Dick!'

A young man came in quickly. He was followed by another. 'Look, it's Dick Wilkins,' said Scrooge to the Ghost. 'Yes, there he is, that's Dick. He liked me very much, did Dick.'

'Hello, my boys,' cried Fezziwig, 'no more work tonight. It's Christmas, Dick! It's Christmas, Ebenezer! Let's close the office.'

You would not believe how fast those two young men worked. They closed all the windows and locked up all the doors as quickly as they could.

'Now,' cried old Fezziwig, jumping down from his desk, 'come along Dick, and you too, Ebenezer. Clear everything away, my boys, and let's have lots of room in here. Quick as you can!'

They cleared away everything while old Fezziwig watched them. It was all done in a minute. Every table and desk was pushed back, as if the room would never be an office again. The floor was brushed and cleaned, the lamps were lit, and plenty of coal was put on the fire. The room was as warm and bright as anyone would wish to see on Christmas Eve, the night before Christmas.

A man came in carrying a violin and a music book. He was followed by Mrs Fezziwig, with a great friendly smile, and the three Miss Fezziwigs, all laughing and beautiful. Then came the six young men who were in love with the three Miss Fezziwigs. Then came all the young men and women who worked in the business. In came the servant with her cousin, then the cook with her brother's best friend. In came the boy from across the road, trying to hide himself behind the girl from the house next door. They all came in, one after another, and started to dance.

Man and woman, boy and girl, twenty pairs all at once, down the middle of the room, back along the sides of the room, up and down the room, round and round the room, most of them usually in the right place, some of them always in the wrong place, but all of them, all the time, laughing and happy and enjoying themselves. When the dance was finished, old Fezziwig clapped his hands and cried out, 'Well done! Well done!' The musician put down his violin and took a long, cool drink.

There were more and more dances. There was cake to eat and there was wine to drink, and there were large pieces of cold meat for those who were very hungry.

After supper, the musician played the best dance of the evening. Old Fezziwig stood up to dance with Mrs Fezziwig. Everyone watched the happy old couple dance alone for a while; then they all started to dance with them.

When the clock struck eleven, the party finished. Mr and Mrs Fezziwig stood on each side of the door. They shook hands with everyone and wished each person a Happy Christmas.

Soon they had all gone and their cheerful voices were no longer heard. The two young men, Dick and Ebenezer, were left to make the room tidy again. But what a party it had been! The best party ever, they thought.

Scrooge puts out the light of Christmas Past

During this time, Scrooge had behaved strangely. His heart seemed to be in the party. He watched the two young men carefully. He remembered everything, enjoyed everything, was excited by the dancing, almost laughed at the jokes. These were very strange things for old Ebenezer Scrooge to do.

He listened to the two young men talking as they tidied the room. They were full of praise for Fezziwig.

They thought he must be the kindest, happiest, most warm-hearted man in the world.

It was not until then that Scrooge remembered the Ghost. He saw that it was looking at him, and that the light on its head was burning very clearly.

'It's not difficult for simple people to be happy,' said the Ghost.

'Simple!' said Scrooge. 'Why do you say they are simple?'

'Well, Fezziwig has only spent a few pounds, three or four perhaps. There is nothing very special about him, is there?'

'It isn't that,' said Scrooge. 'It isn't that, Ghost. Fezziwig was able to make us happy or sad; he was able to make our work heavy or light. He did so many kind things for us. Perhaps they were all very small things and perhaps they cost him very little. But that was not important. The happiness he gave us was so wonderful. It meant more to us than anything he might have bought with a lot of money.' And then he stopped, as if he was surprised to hear himself saying such things.

He felt the Ghost's eyes looking at him.

'What's the matter?' asked the Ghost.

'Oh, nothing at all!' said Scrooge.

'Something, I think.'

'No,' said Scrooge, 'but I would like to say a few words to my clerk, Bob Cratchit, right now. That's all.'

As he made this wish, the young Scrooge started turning out the lights in Fezziwig's office.

'These are the shadows of things in your past,' said the Ghost. 'You have not thought of them for a long time, but they are part of you.'

'Take me away,' cried Scrooge, 'show me no more.' He felt strangely sad.

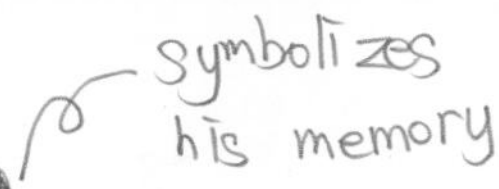

The Ghost's light was burning high and bright. Quickly, Scrooge took hold of the pointed cap and covered the ghost's head. The Ghost dropped to the floor, but the light of Christmas Past still shone from under the cap. Scrooge pushed the cap down and down, harder and harder. But as much as he tried he could not stop it. The light kept shining out.

He began to feel tired. He also felt quite weak. He sat down on the floor to take a rest. The last light went out in Fezziwig's office. Suddenly the Ghost was gone, and it grew very dark.

He looked around and about. At first he could see nothing. Then, slowly, as his eyes got used to the dark, he began to see shapes. A large old bed, a cupboard for clothes, a window to the right of it. Then, to his surprise, he knew where he was. He was sitting on the floor in his own bedroom again. He got back into bed and fell into a deep sleep.

7
The Ghost of Christmas Present

When Scrooge woke up, he knew that it was almost one o'clock. He felt that he had woken up just in time. He was ready for anything.

He heard the church clock strike one.

Nothing happened. No ghost appeared. Five minutes, ten minutes, a quarter of an hour passed and no one came. He did not know what to think.

But then he noticed that his bedroom was not as dark as it should have been. There seemed to be some light coming in from somewhere. He looked about, and saw that it was coming from the next room, his sitting room.

When he saw it, this light frightened him more than a thousand ghosts, but he wanted to know what was causing it. He got up, put his slippers on his feet, and moved very quietly across the floor to the door of his sitting room.

'Come in, Ebenezer Scrooge,' called a large, loud, friendly voice. Scrooge jumped with fear. He had not even touched the door. How did anyone know he was there?

But he obeyed the voice. Very gently he pushed the door open a little, and looked in.

He could not believe what he saw. It was his own sitting room, but it had changed. It looked like a garden. The walls and ceiling were covered with dark green leaves, and among the leaves were hundreds of shining red berries — the fruit of the holly. A great fire was burning — something no one had ever seen in that room the whole time Scrooge had lived there. On the tables and all over the floor there were heaps of Christmas food — meat, fruit, cakes, and sweets — and large cups of warm wine to drink. A very big, tall, happy man was sitting on a great chair in the middle of it all. It was wonderful to see the room like this, and it was even more wonderful to see that big, happy man with all those things around him. He carried a bright light, and held it up high as Scrooge came round the door.

'Come in, come in!' cried the ghost, in his loud, friendly voice. 'Come in, and get to know me better, my friend.'

Scrooge entered. He did not know what else to do. He was so frightened. In his fear he stood in front of this ghost, his eyes looking down at his feet. The ghost's eyes were clear and kind, but Scrooge was too frightened to look at them.

'I am the Ghost of Christmas Present,' said the big man. 'Look at me.'

Scrooge did as the Ghost said. He saw that the ghost was a strong-looking person. It was wearing a long green coat with white around the bottom. Its feet and chest were not covered with anything, but it did not seem to be cold. On its head there were some

green leaves, and bright red holly berries and pieces of shining white ice. It had long, dark brown hair, a kind face, laughing eyes, and a great, happy voice.

'Have you ever seen anyone like me before?' asked the Ghost.

'Never,' answered Scrooge.

'Really? I am surprised! Have you never spent some time with other members of my family? With my brother of last year, perhaps, or my brother of the year before that?'

'I don't think I have,' said Scrooge. 'No, I am afraid I haven't. Have you got many brothers, Ghost?'

'Nearly two thousand.'

'That is a large family,' thought Scrooge. 'It must cost a lot of money to buy food for them all.'

As he talked to the Ghost, Scrooge began to feel a little less frightened. But not much.

He remembered the Ghost of Christmas Past. He thought that this new ghost would want to show him something, too.

'Ghost,' said Scrooge, 'please take me anywhere you want. The Ghost of Christmas Past showed me things in my life that I had forgotten. I learnt much from that. I learnt that I might have been a kinder, better man. Tonight, if you have anything to teach me, I hope I shall learn something from you, too.'

The kind eyes of the Ghost of Christmas Present looked straight at Scrooge, and smiled.

'Touch my coat,' it said.

Scrooge did as he was told, and held on to the Ghost's coat tightly.

Christmas present

The room, the fire, the meat, the fruit, the cakes, the sweets, the dark green holly leaves, the bright red holly berries, all went in a second. Scrooge and the ghost were outside, standing in the light of a cold winter's day.

They were in a street in London. It was Christmas morning. There was snow everywhere. When people stepped on it, their boots made a rough, pleasant, crunching noise as they walked along. They brushed the snow from the paths in front of their homes, and threw it down from the house tops. Little boys thought it was great fun to watch the snow falling down into the road below, and breaking up into small white clouds when it hit the ground.

The street itself was not very bright, but there was happiness everywhere. The people who were clearing the snow from their houses were full of fun. They called out to each other as they brushed the snow away. Sometimes they threw snowballs at each other. They laughed if their snowballs hit the wrong person, and they laughed even more if they hit the right one.

The shop windows were full of light and colour. There were fat birds hanging in the meat shops, chickens and ducks, geese and turkeys. Every bird was ready to be taken home and cooked for Christmas dinner. If they were too big to be cooked at home, they could be cooked in the kitchens of the bakers' shops.

In the fruit shops there were heaps of oranges and lemons, apples and pears, with so many bright colours, — red, green, orange and yellow. All were ready for carrying home in paper bags to eat after dinner. In other shops, you could smell the tea and the coffee, and that smell was mixed with the smell of cakes and puddings,

all full of good things to eat, and looking very sweet. The smell was so good that even if a person were very hungry, he might soon think he had already eaten too much!

The people in the shops were hurrying about and looking very busy, buying all the things they needed to be happy at Christmas. Some left their parcels in the shops and came running back to get them. Sometimes they banged against each other in the shop doorways, dropping their bags and parcels on to the floor. If that made them angry with each other, the Ghost would run to them and wave his light over their heads. They would soon be laughing. They would think to themselves that it was not possible to argue on Christmas Day.

8
Christmas at Bob Cratchit's

Scrooge was beginning to feel kind towards all the people he could see, but the Ghost moved on, taking Scrooge with him. He took him straight to Camden Town, to the house of his clerk, Bob Cratchit.

They went inside. They saw Bob's wife, Mrs Cratchit. Her clothes were poor, but she was dressed in bright, cheerful colours. She laid the cloth on the table, helped by Belinda, her second daughter. Young Peter Cratchit stuck a fork into the cooking pot and tried to taste the food that was cooking there.

Two smaller Cratchits, a boy and a girl, came running in. They said that they had been to the baker's and they had smelt the Cratchit's goose cooking there in the baker's kitchen. It had made them think of the good dinner they were going to have! These two smaller Cratchits danced around the table. Master Peter blew on the fire until the food in the pot boiled.

'Now, where is your father?' called Mrs Cratchit. 'And your brother, Tiny Tim? And Martha? Where is she? She was not as late as this last Christmas.'

'Here's Martha, Mother,' said Martha, appearing in the doorway as she spoke.

'Here's Martha, Mother,' repeated the two smaller Cratchits. 'Martha! Martha! The goose is so big!'

'God bless you, dear!' said Mrs Cratchit, kissing Martha many times and taking off her coat and hat. 'You're so late!'

'We had a lot of work to finish last night,' replied the girl, 'and we had to clear away this morning, Mother.'

'Well, that does not matter now. I am just happy that you've come. Sit down by the fire for a minute and make yourself warm.'

'No, no, here's Father coming,' cried the two smaller Cratchits, who were everywhere at once. 'Hide, Martha, hide.'

So Martha hid herself, and Bob came in.

Bob Cratchit, husband of Mrs Cratchit and father of all the other Cratchits, came in with his long scarf hanging down in front of him. His thin clothes were mended and brushed because it was Christmas Day. Sitting on his shoulders was a thin little boy.

Since he was a baby, this child had never been well. He had only grown very slowly. Because of this everyone called him Tiny Tim.

Poor Tiny Tim was not strong enough to run about like other children. There were pieces of iron around his legs, and he had to use a stick to help him walk.

'Why, where's our Martha?' cried Bob Cratchit, looking round. 'Hasn't she come yet?'

'She's not coming,' said Mrs Cratchit, joining in the game.

'Not coming?' said Bob, suddenly looking unhappy. He had pretended to be a horse for Tim all the way from church, and had come home in great joy. 'Isn't she coming to see us on Christmas Day?'

Martha did not like to see her father looking sad, even though it was only a joke. She came out from behind the door, and ran into his arms.

The two smaller Cratchits carried Tiny Tim into the kitchen. They wanted to show him the pot with the Christmas pudding cooking in it. They wanted him to listen to it banging against the pot as it boiled.

'Did Tim behave well at church?' asked Mrs Cratchit, when Bob had kissed his daughter and talked to her.

'Very well,' replied Bob. 'You know he has many thoughts sitting by himself so much. He thinks the strangest things you have ever heard. He told me something when we were coming home. He said he hoped the people saw him in church, because they would see he could not walk easily. He wanted them to enjoy thinking about God, who helps people who are poor and ill.'

Bob's voice was not calm when he told them this. It was not calm, either, when he said that he thought Tiny Tim was growing stronger.

Tiny Tim came back from the kitchen, with his brother and sister, to his chair by the fire. Bob, taking off his hat, mixed a hot drink in a jug, and put it near the fire. Young Peter and the two younger Cratchits went to fetch the goose. They soon returned.

Then they set places at the table for everyone, not forgetting themselves. Bob made Tiny Tim sit next to him at a corner of the table. At last the dishes were put out on the table, and the family gave their thanks to God for the food they were going to eat.

Then came an exciting time, as Mrs Cratchit started to cut up the goose. When she did this, a sound of joy was heard all round. Even Tiny Tim, excited by the two young Cratchits, hit the table with his knife and cried 'Hurrah!'

They had never had a goose as big as this one, they said to each other, happily. Bob said he did not believe there ever could be another goose as big as this. It was enough to feed the whole family.

After they had eaten, Mrs Cratchit looked at the dish where the goose had been. She said she was happy that there were just a few pieces left! Everyone said they had eaten enough, and the plates were changed by Miss Belinda.

Mrs Cratchit then went into the kitchen alone. She would not let anyone come with her because she did not wish them to see what she was doing there. It was time to bring in the Christmas pudding.

The two young Cratchits went pale when they thought about all the things that might go wrong. Was it cooked enough? Would it break when their mother took it from the pot and put it on the dish? Had some robbers climbed over the wall and stolen it while they were eating the goose?

What a lot of steam! The pudding came out of the pot. There was a smell like washing-day! That was the cloth around the pudding.

Then there was a smell like a baker's shop. That was the pudding. It was dark brown with many small, black, pieces of fruit that had been cooked in it.

Mrs Cratchit put the pudding on a dish. The pudding did not break. She poured wine all over it. She carefully put a small piece of holly on the top. She took a piece of paper, lit it from the fire, and then set fire to the wine. The pudding was covered with beautiful blue flames! Now, it was ready!

In half a minute Mrs Cratchit came back, carrying high the Christmas pudding which was bright with the flames of the burning wine. She was quite red in the face, but she smiled proudly.

'Oh, what a wonderful pudding!' Bob said, and he meant it too. It was the best Christmas pudding Mrs Cratchit had made since they were first married. Everyone had something to say about it. Nobody said that they thought it was quite a small pudding for such a large family. No Cratchit would even think of such a thing!

At last the dinner was finished. The cloth was cleared and the fire made up. The drink which Bob had mixed was tasted; it was just right.

Apples and pears were put on the table. All the family sat round the fire in what Bob called a circle, but he meant half a circle. At his side were the family glasses — two large glasses and a large cup. They thought that these held the hot drink better than cups of gold. Bob poured it for them with a smiling face, and then said, 'A Happy Christmas to us all, my dears, God bless us!' And the family said the same.

Will Tiny Tim live?

'God bless us all,' said Tiny Tim the youngest person in the family. He sat upon his little chair, very close to his father. Bob held his hand because he loved the child and wished to keep him by his side. He was afraid that God might take him from this world.

'Ghost,' said Scrooge, with an interest he had never felt before, 'tell me if Tiny Tim will live.'

'I see an empty chair in the corner, and a small stick without its owner,' replied the Ghost, sadly. 'If there is no change in the future, the child will die.'

'No, no,' said Scrooge, 'oh no, kind Ghost, say that he will live.'

'If next Christmas we do not find him here, what then? It does not matter, does it, Ebenezer Scrooge? If he is too weak to live, he must die. Then the numbers of the poor will grow less.'

Scrooge hung his head when he heard his own words said again by the ghost. But he looked up quickly when he heard someone calling out his own name.

'Mr Scrooge!' said Bob. He was holding up one of the glasses of warm wine. 'We will drink in the name of Mr Scrooge who gave us the dinner.'

'Gave us the dinner?' said Mrs Cratchit, going very red. 'I wish he were here. I would give him a few things to think about.'

'My dear,' said Bob, 'it is Christmas Day!'

'I will drink to his health because you want me to and because today is Christmas Day, but not because of him. Long life, a Happy Christmas and a Happy New Year, to Mr Scrooge! But I don't know how he can ever be very joyful, or very happy!'

The children drank after her. It was the first thing they had done that day without joy. Tiny Tim drank the last of all. The name of Scrooge had made them sad. They were quiet for five minutes. But then, after a little while, after they had finished thinking about Scrooge, they were ten times happier than before.

They were not a good-looking family. They were not well-dressed; their shoes did not keep out the wet weather; their clothes were poor and thin. But they were happy and kind and pleased to be with one another. Scrooge watched them all, especially Tiny Tim.

'Come,' said the Ghost. 'We have another visit to make.'

9

Christmas at Scrooge's Nephew's House

By this time it was getting dark, and there was a lot of snow falling. As Scrooge and the Ghost went along the streets, the bright flames of the fires in the houses were wonderful to see. Children were running out to be the first to greet their married sisters, brothers, uncles, and aunts. Many people were on their way to friendly parties.

What a kind ghost! He led Scrooge to where men worked deep down in the earth, and to those out in country fields. Even to ships sailing across the sea, where sailors sang their Christmas songs, and remembered those they loved so far away.

While Scrooge was thinking about these sights, he heard a loud, happy laugh. It was a great surprise to him. It was his nephew's laugh. Then he found himself in a bright room. The ghost was smiling by his side, and looking with joy at the nephew.

'Ha, ha, ha,' laughed Scrooge's nephew. 'Ha, ha, ha!' And all his friends laughed with him.

They talk about Scrooge

'He said that Christmas was nonsense,' cried Scrooge's nephew, 'and he believed it too!'

'Well, I hope he will be sorry for thinking such things, Fred,' said Scrooge's niece.

She was very pretty, with a gentle, surprised-looking face, a sweet little mouth, and the loveliest eyes you ever saw.

'He's a strange old man,' said Scrooge's nephew, 'that's true, and he's not really very pleasant either. However, he punishes himself by his own bad habits, and I have nothing to say against him.'

'I'm sure he's very rich, Fred,' said Scrooge's niece.

'That isn't important, my dear,' said Scrooge's nephew. 'His money is of no use to him. He doesn't do any good with it. He doesn't even make himself happy with it. And he has not the joy of thinking that it will ever help me.'

'Well, I do not like him, and I hope I never have to see him,' said Scrooge's niece. Scrooge's niece's sisters and all the other ladies thought the same.

'Oh, I wouldn't say that,' said Scrooge's nephew. 'I am sorry for him. If I really tried I would be angry with him. But he just makes himself sad because of his own bad ways. He decides not to like us, so he won't come to dinner with us. What happens? Nothing at all happens to us, and he just loses a dinner. It wasn't very good dinner, either, so he didn't lose much!'

'I think he lost a wonderful dinner,' said Scrooge's niece. Everyone else said the same, and they were right. They had finished dinner, and, with the wine and sweets and fruit upon the table, they were sitting round the fire in the lamplight.

'Well, I'm glad to hear you say so,' said Scrooge's nephew, 'because I thought our new cook was not a very good cook! What do you think, Topper?'

Topper answered that he did not know much about cooking because he was not married. As he said this he looked at one of Scrooge's niece's sisters, the fat one in the silk dress, not the pretty one. Her face went quite red.

'Do go on, Fred,' said Scrooge's niece. 'He never finishes what he begins to say,' she said to the other sister.

Scrooge's nephew enjoyed another loud laugh, and everyone else laughed too.

'I was going to say,' he went on, 'that because he does not like to be happy with us, it is he who loses, not us. He loses some pleasant hours which could only make him happy. I am sure we would be better friends to him than he can find living alone, either in his dark old office or in his dark old house. I want to ask him here every year, whether he likes it or not, because I am sorry for him. Even if he hates Christmas until he dies, I hope he will think a little better of it through me. I shall go there year after year saying, "Uncle Scrooge, how are you?" If that makes him leave his poor clerk fifty pounds it will have done some good. You know, I think what I said yesterday made him think.'

They laughed again. How could anyone change old Scrooge! But they were all quite kind. They did not care much what they laughed at, but they did like laughing.

After supper they had some music, for they loved singing together. Topper could sing the deep sounds without getting red in the face. Scrooge's niece played the piano well. She played a simple little song which Scrooge had known at school.

When he heard this music, Scrooge thought about all the things that the ghost had shown him. He became less and less hard, less and less cold-hearted. He wished he had listened to this music more often, years ago. Why had he made his own life so sad for so long?

But they did not give the whole evening to music. They played games, for it is good for grown people to be like children sometimes, especially at Christmas.

Christmas games

They played a game called blind man's buff. One person has a scarf tied round his eyes. He cannot see. He is like a blind man.

Then he must move about the room and try to catch someone else. If he catches another person, he must guess that person's name. Then, if he is right, he can take the scarf off and the other person must put it on.

When Topper was the 'blind man', it is hard to believe that he really could not see through the scarf. You should have seen the way he went after that fat sister in the silk dress! He knocked over the table, fell over the chairs and hit the piano. But everywhere she went, he went too. He always knew where that sister was! He would not catch anyone else. Some of them fell against him, but he did not catch them! He went away at once following the fat sister. She often cried out that it was not right to do that, and it really was not. And when at last he caught her, he pretended he did not know who she was!

The Ghost was very pleased to find Scrooge so interested. He was happy to hear him ask, like a child, to stay until the end of the party. 'Here is a new game,' said Scrooge. 'One half-hour more, Ghost, please!'

It was a game called Yes and No. Scrooge's nephew had to think of something, and the rest must find out what he was thinking. He could only answer Yes or No to their questions.

He was asked many questions. They found that he was thinking of an animal. A living animal; an animal which was not kind; not a gentle animal; an angry animal; an animal that talked sometimes; lived in London and walked along the streets; not led about by anybody; did not live in a zoo; did not like Christmas but was never killed in a market; it was not a goose or a duck, not a horse, a donkey, a cow, a tiger, a dog, a pig, or a cat.

Every time a question was put to him, this nephew laughed again. He was so amused that he had to stand up. At last the fat sister in the silk dress called out, 'I have found it, Fred, I know what it is.'

'What is it?' asked Fred.

'It's your Uncle Scroo-o-o-oge.'

And it certainly was. Everyone thought Scrooge's nephew was very clever. Some now said that the answer to 'Is it a tiger?' should have been 'Yes', because old Scrooge was like an angry old tiger!

'He has given us plenty of fun, I'm sure,' said Fred, 'and so we should drink to his health. Here is a glass of wine, I drink to the health of Uncle Scrooge.'

'To Uncle Scrooge!' they all cried.

'A Happy Christmas, and a Happy New Year to the old man, even if he is an old tiger,' said Scrooge's nephew. 'He would not take my "Happy Christmas" from me, but all the same, I give it to him. Happy Christmas, Uncle Scrooge!'

Scrooge had become happy with these young people. He wanted to thank them. But he had forgotten that no one could hear him, and the Ghost said there was no more time. The whole room went dark. The Ghost and Scrooge were again on their travels.

The Ghost grows older

They saw much and they went far. They visited many homes, but always there was happiness. The Ghost stood at the side of people who were ill and they became cheerful. He stood by people in countries that were far away, and they seemed closer to home. He stood by poor men and they felt rich. He went to hospitals, and prisons, and poorhouses, and left his happiness everywhere.

It was a long night. But Scrooge was not sure if it was only one night. He thought one thing was very strange. His face and body did not change, but he could see that the Ghost was growing older.

'Is your life so short?' asked Scrooge. He looked at the Ghost as they stood together in an open space, and he noticed that its hair was white.

'My life upon this earth is very short,' replied the Ghost. 'It began not long before we met, and it ends tonight.'

'Tonight!' cried Scrooge. 'Just one day?'

'Tonight, at midnight; the time is coming close.'

They heard the church clock striking a quarter to midnight. Not long after that, the clock struck twelve.

Scrooge looked about him for the Ghost, and did not see it.

On the last sound of the bell, he remembered that Jacob Marley had told him there would be a third ghost. He saw something in the distance. It was covered from head to foot in black. It was moving like a dark cloud, along the ground towards him.

10
The Ghost of Christmas Yet to Come

Scrooge was, by now, used to ghosts. But he was very much afraid of this silent shape. His legs shook and felt very weak. He could hardly stand when he tried to follow it. The ghost waited a minute to give him more time.

But Scrooge felt even worse. He was filled with fear because he knew that under the black clothes there were eyes which could see him. Although he looked very hard, he himself could see nothing but a black shape, and the ghost's hand.

'Are you the Ghost of Christmas Yet to Come?' he asked. 'I fear you more than any ghost I have seen. But I know that your purpose is to do me good, and I hope to become a better man than I was. I shall come with you, and I come with a thankful heart. Will you not speak to me?'

The Ghost said nothing. Its hand was pointed straight in front of him.

'I come, then,' said Scrooge, 'I come. The night is passing quickly, and time is short for me. Lead on, Ghost.'

The Ghost moved past Scrooge. Scrooge followed in the shadow of its coat. He thought that the ghost lifted him up and carried him along.

Who has died?

After a very short time, they were standing in the centre of London, near Scrooge's office. Businessmen hurried up and down the street, and looked carefully at their watches, as Scrooge had often seen them do. Three were standing together, talking.

'No,' said a great fat man to a very thin man, 'I don't know much about it. I only know he's dead.'

'When did he die?'

'Last night, I believe.'

'Why, what was the matter with him?' asked a third man. 'I thought he would never die.'

'Who knows?' said the first.

'What has he done with all his money?' asked another man, one with a very red face.

'I have not heard,' said the first man. 'Given it to his business, perhaps. He hasn't left it to me. I know that!'

The other two laughed at the joke loudly.

'His funeral is tomorrow,' said the same man. 'I don't

know if anyone will go. It will be very cheap. Perhaps we should go.'

'I don't mind if there is some food. I must eat well if I go to a funeral.'

They all laughed again.

The three men walked away in different directions and mixed with other people in the street. Scrooge knew the men, but he did not know what they were talking about. He looked to the ghost, hoping it would tell him, but it said nothing.

Scrooge has gone away

The Ghost went on into another street, closer to *Scrooge and Marley's*. Its finger pointed to two people, and Scrooge listened again. He knew these men also. They were businessmen, rich and important. Scrooge always hoped that they would think he was a good businessman.

'How are you?' said one.

'How are you?' replied the other.

'So, old Scratch has died at last.'

'I have heard,' answered the other. 'Cold, isn't it?'

'It usually is at Christmas. Are you going anywhere special for the holiday?'

'No, I have something else to do. Good morning.'

'Good morning.'

Scrooge was puzzled. He had never heard of anyone called 'Old Scratch'.

Just then a clock struck half past ten. Every day, at exactly half past ten, Scrooge left his office and went out to drink coffee and to read the morning newspapers. He always walked along this street. He was never any earlier, never any later, and he never went along any other street.

He looked for himself. He thought if he saw himself, then he would understand what his future life would be. But Ebenezer Scrooge did not appear.

Scrooge did not know what to think. Then he remembered something. He had often thought that in the future he would stop doing his business. He planned to sell everything, and go and live away from London.

So it was all quite clear. He was seeing the future now, and he could not see himself because he had gone away.

The Ghost led him through many more streets. Scrooge looked here and there to find himself. He was nowhere to be seen, but that did not worry him any longer.

The old clothes shop

After going a long way, they were still in London, but Scrooge did not know where. The streets were narrow and dirty, the houses small, dark, and crowded with poor people. Scrooge had never been in that part of London before.

They went into a small shop. It was dark inside. The shop was full of things that people had thrown away, or which were not wanted any longer. Many of the things were torn and dirty. The shop smelt very bad.

The door opened, and a woman walked in with a large bag. She put the bag on the floor, and sat on it. Half a minute later a second woman came in, also carrying a large bag. Then, just a few seconds after that, in came a thin man with a small bag. All three looked at each other in surprise, and then began to laugh.

The shopkeeper came to see what the noise was about.

'Look, old Joe,' said the woman who had come in first, 'isn't it strange? We have all been at the same business, and we have all come here at the same time, but not one of us knew what the others were doing!'

'Well, you have come to the right place,' said old Joe. 'Now, let me see what you have brought.'

Scrooge watched. He wanted to know what business they had been doing. It soon became clear.

The man worked for an undertaker. He had been sent to the house of a man who had died. His job was to measure the body, and get everything ready for the funeral. But while he was there he had taken some of the dead man's things. He had not taken much, just some silver buttons, and a small piece of jewellery.

One of the women worked as a cleaner. She had been to the same house, and taken some things, too. She had taken sheets and towels, a few clothes and some shoes.

The laundress

The other woman had been the dead man's laundress. When he was alive, she washed his clothes for him. Now she opened her bag.

'What are these, then?' said old Joe, in surprise. 'Curtains? Not bed-curtains?'

'Bed-curtains,' said the woman.

'You didn't take them from the bed while he was in it?' said old Joe, even more surprised.

'I did! Why not? He wasn't going to tell me not to!' the woman replied.

'You were born to be rich,' said old Joe, smiling at her, 'and you will be before long.'

'Well, I shan't stop myself from trying. Not while there are people like him in this world. He only cared about himself when he was alive. Why shouldn't we help ourselves to some of his things when he is dead? He won't need them any longer.'

The others all agreed with her.

'And what are these?' asked old Joe, taking the curtains away and finding more things underneath.

'Blankets,' said the woman.

'His blankets?' asked Joe.

'No one else's,' said the woman. 'You are not worrying that he will feel cold without them, are you?'

They all laughed. Then she showed them a white shirt.

'Look at it,' she said. 'That is as good as new. That is his best shirt. There isn't a hole in it anywhere. If I had not taken it, it would have been wasted.'

'What do you mean by "wasted"?' asked old Joe.

'Someone had put it on him, and he was going to be buried in it. But I took it off again and put an old one on him. He won't look any uglier in that one!'

Old Joe took out some money, and paid each one of them.

'This is how it ends,' the woman laughed. 'When he was alive he frightened everyone away from him. Now he is dead there is no one to care about him, and we can make some money.'

They all laughed again, but Scrooge, watching and listening, thought only of the poor dead man. He had died alone and without any friends. There was no one to stop these people taking his things.

'Ghost,' he said. 'I think I understand. This poor man's life was rather like my own.'

Suddenly the shop disappeared.

11
Tiny Tim is Dead

They went back through the streets, all the way across London to Bob Cratchit's house. They went in and found the mother and the children sitting round the fire.

It was quiet. Very quiet. The noisy little Cratchits were not noisy any longer. They were quite still in one corner, and sat looking up at Peter. Peter had a book on his knees. The mother and her daughters were sewing. They were all very quiet.

'And he set a little child among them.'

The words were in Scrooge's head. How had he heard them? He had not dreamed them, had he? Did the boy read them out as he and the Ghost entered the house? Why did he not read some more?

The mother laid her work on the table and put her hands to her face. 'The colour is bad for my eyes,' she said. 'It makes them weak in the lamplight. I wouldn't like your father to see me like this when he comes home. It is nearly time for him to come, now, isn't it?'

'Past it, I think,' said Peter, shutting up his book, 'but he walks a little slower these days, Mother.'

They were very quiet again. At last she said, and in a cheerful voice, 'I have known him walk very fast, carrying Tiny Tim.'

'I have also, often,' cried Peter.

'And we too,' said everyone else.

'But he was so very light to carry,' she went on, 'and his father loved him. It was no trouble, no trouble. Listen! Here is your father at the door, now.'

Mrs Cratchit hurried to meet him, and Bob with his scarf, which he needed because it was so cold, came in. His tea was ready for him by the fire, and they all tried to help him with it. Then the two young Cratchits climbed on to his knees and laid their faces against his. They did not speak, but they wanted to say, 'Don't be sad, Father.'

Bob was very cheerful with them and spoke very pleasantly to all the family.

'I wish you had come with me this afternoon, my dear,' Bob said to his wife. 'You would have been so happy to see how green the place is. But then you'll see it often. I promised him we would walk there every Sunday.'

Then, suddenly, he began to cry. He couldn't help it. 'My little, little child,' he said, 'my poor little child.'

They sat by the fire and talked, the girls and the mother still sewing. Bob told them of the kindness of Mr Scrooge's nephew, whom he had only seen once before. The nephew had stopped him in the street that day, and seeing that he looked a little sad, he had asked Bob what was the matter.

'Then,' said Bob, 'I told him. "I am very sorry about it, Mr Cratchit," he said to me, "and I am very sorry for your good wife." I don't know how he knew that.'

'Knew what, my dear?'

'That you were a good wife.'

'Everyone knows that,' said Peter.

'Very well said, my boy,' said Bob. 'I hope they do.' Then he continued, '"I am very sorry for your good wife," Mr Scrooge's nephew said to me. "If I can be of help to you in any way," he said, giving me his card, "that's where I live. Please come to see me." Now it wasn't because of anything he might do for me. It was more because of his kind heart, I think. I felt he had known our Tiny Tim and that his thoughts were with us.'

'I'm sure he's a good man,' said Mrs Cratchit.

'You would be more sure of it, my dear,' said Bob, 'if you saw and spoke to him. I would not be surprised if he gets Peter a better job.'

'Did you hear that, Peter?' said Mrs Cratchit.

'Well,' said Bob, 'I am sure none of us shall ever forget Tiny Tim, shall we, or this first "goodbye" that there was among us?'

'Never, Father,' they all cried.

'And I know, my dears,' said Bob, 'that we remember how patient and gentle he was, although he was just a little child. We shall not argue easily among ourselves, and forget poor Tiny Tim in doing it.'

'No, never, Father,' they all cried again.

'I am very happy,' said Bob. 'I am very happy.'

Mrs Cratchit kissed him, his daughters kissed him, the two young Cratchits kissed him, and Peter and he shook hands.

Scrooge learns the name of the dead man

'Ghost,' said Scrooge, sadly, 'something tells me that the hour when we must leave is near. I know it, but I don't know how. Tell me the name of the man whose death was spoken about.'

The Ghost of Christmas Yet to Come moved forward. It reached the street where Scrooge's business house was. As they passed, Scrooge looked through the window. The man sitting in his chair was not himself.

He followed the Ghost until they reached a high gate. He looked round before entering. A cemetery! The man whose name he was going to learn must be here, he thought.

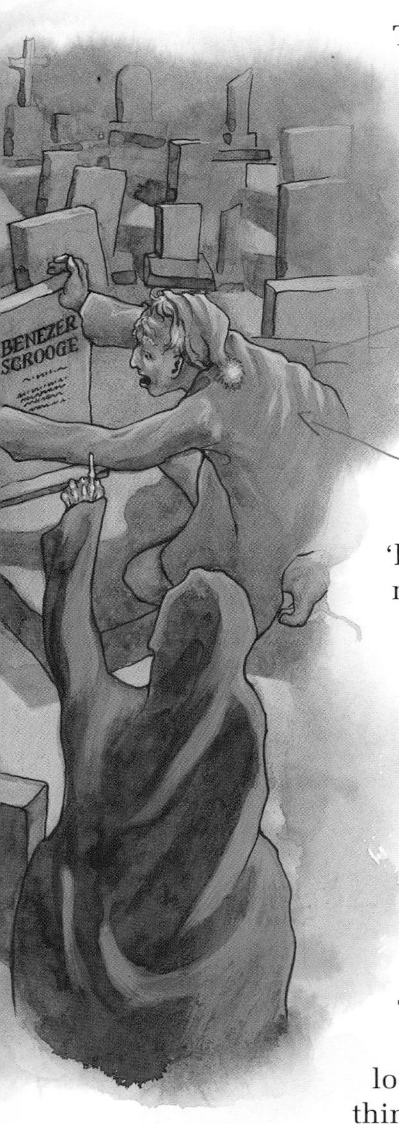

The Ghost stood among the gravestones and pointed down to one. Scrooge went nearer. He shook with fear as he went. Following the Ghost's finger, he read upon the stone his own name, EBENEZER SCROOGE.

The finger pointed from the grave to him and back again.

'No, Ghost! Oh no, no, no!'

The Ghost said nothing.

'Ghost,' cried Scrooge, 'listen to me. I am not the man I was. Why do you show me this if there is no hope for me?'

For the first time the hand of the Ghost appeared to shake.

'Good Ghost,' Scrooge went on, 'you are sorry for me. Tell me that I can still change what you have shown me, by living a new life.'

The kind hand shook again.

'I shall love Christmas and look forward to it, and try to think of it all the year. I will live in the past, the present, and the future. I will not shut out the lessons that they teach. Oh tell me that I can rub out the writing on this stone.'

In his pain he took hold of the Ghost's hand. The Ghost tried to pull free. But Scrooge held on as tightly as he could, all the time crying out to the Ghost that he would be a better man.

Then it seemed to him that it had grown lighter. His voice was louder. What was happening? Where was he? He looked at the Ghost's hand. It was made of wood. It did not look like a hand at all; it was just a piece of wood. He looked around him. He was holding on to the wooden part of his own bed, in his own bedroom. The room was filled with the light of the morning sun.

12
Scrooge Wakes Up on Christmas Morning

Yes, what he had thought was the Ghost's hand was really part of a bed, and the bed was his own bed, and the room was his own room. Best of all, the time before him was his own time.

'I will live in the past, the present, and the future,' he said again, as he jumped up. 'Oh, Jacob Marley, I thank heaven and Christmas time for this. I say it on my knees, old Jacob, on my knees.'

He was so full of his new ideas that he could hardly speak. In his last minutes with the ghost he had been crying and his face was wet with tears. He was busy putting on his clothes as he laughed through his tears. 'I am as happy as a child. I am as cheerful as a schoolboy. A Happy Christmas to everyone. A Happy New Year to all the world.'

He danced into his other room. 'Ha, ha, ha!' he laughed, and for a man who had not laughed for so many years it was a very good laugh. The first of many, many very good laughs. 'I don't know what day it is,' he cried. 'I don't know anything. Hello there!' Running to the window he opened it, and put out his head — a clear cold day, fresh air, and bright, beautiful sunlight.

'What's today?' cried Scrooge, calling down to a boy who was dressed in his best clothes.

'What did you say?' replied the boy.

'What's today, my fine friend?' said Scrooge again.

'Today?' replied the boy. 'It's Christmas Day, of course!'

'It's Christmas Day,' said Scrooge to himself, 'and I have not missed it. The ghosts all came in one night. Well, they can do anything they like, ghosts can.' Then he shouted to the boy again, 'Hello, my fine friend.'

'Hello,' replied the boy.

'Do you know the shop with the fine turkey in the next street?'

'Of course I do,' replied the boy.

'A fine boy! A clever boy!' Scrooge said to himself. Then, to the boy, 'Have they sold the turkey which was hanging there? Not the little one, the big one?'

'What, the one as big as me?'

'Such a wonderful boy,' thought Scrooge. 'It's so pleasant to talk to him.' And he shouted, 'Yes, the big one.'

'It's hanging there now,' said the boy.

'Is it? Go and buy it.'

'You're joking,' cried the boy.

'No, no, I am serious. Go and buy it. Tell them to bring it here, so that I can tell them where to take it. Come back with the man, and I'll give you some money. Come back with him in less than five minutes and I'll give you three times as much.'

The boy ran off at once.

'I'll send it to Bob Cratchit,' Scrooge said to himself, 'and he won't know who has sent it.'

The boy soon returned with a man carrying a very large turkey.

'It's not possible to carry that all the way to Camden Town. You must take a carriage,' Scrooge said to the man.

He laughed as he said this, he laughed as he paid the boy, and he laughed as he paid for the turkey. He even laughed as he paid for the carriage. Everything about him gave him happiness.

Scrooge gives to the poor

He dressed himself in his best clothes, and at last got into the street. He had not gone far when he met the gentleman who had walked into his office the day before, asking for money for the poor.

'My dear sir,' Scrooge said, taking the man by both his hands, 'how do you do? I hope you had a successful day yesterday. And I, too, would like to give a little. If it is not too late, would you please allow me to give you — ' here Scrooge whispered into his ear.

'Good heavens!' cried the gentleman, very surprised. 'Mr Scrooge, are you serious?'

'If you please,' said Scrooge, 'I shall give nothing less.'

'My dear sir,' said the other, shaking Scrooge by the hand, 'I do not know what to say to such kindness.'

'Don't say anything, please. I am grateful to you and I thank you fifty times. Come and see me, please. Come and see me another day, will you?'

'I will,' said the gentleman. 'Oh yes, Mr Scrooge, I will.'

Scrooge went to church, and then he watched the people going up and down in the streets. In the afternoon he went to his nephew's house. He passed the door twelve times because he was afraid to knock, but at last he did it.

Scroogе visits his nephew

'Is your master at home, my dear?' he said to the girl.

'He's in the dining room.'

'Thank you, he knows me,' said Scrooge, with his hand on the dining room door. 'I'll go in.'

He opened the door quietly, and first put his head round the door. His nephew and niece were looking at the table to see that everything was right.

'Fred!' said Scrooge.

They were so surprised! 'Good heavens!' cried Fred. 'Who's that?'

'It's I, your Uncle Scrooge. I've come to dinner. May I come in?'

They were so pleased to see him that Scrooge nearly had his hand shaken off. He felt at home in five minutes. Everyone looked just the same when they came in as when Scrooge had seen them with the ghost. It was a wonderful party! Wonderful games! Wonderful happiness!

The next day

Scrooge went to the office early the next morning. He wanted to catch Bob coming late. That was what he wanted to do most. And he did it. The clock struck nine, no Bob! A quarter past! No Bob! Bob was a full eighteen minutes late. Scrooge sat with his door wide open where he could see him come in.

Bob sat on his stool without wasting a second, and began writing very fast.

'Hello,' Scrooge called in his usual voice (or as near as he could make it), 'what do you mean by coming at this time of the day?'

'I am sorry,' said Bob. 'I am late.'

'Oh, you are, yes, I think you are very late. Come in here, please.'

'It is only once a year,' cried Bob, 'and it will not happen again. I was very happy yesterday.'

'Now, I'll tell you something, my friend,' said Scrooge. 'I am not going to allow this any longer.' He jumped from his chair and took hold of Bob's arm, 'and therefore, I am going to increase your pay.'

Bob nearly fell over; he was so surprised. He reached for his ruler, thinking that old Scrooge was going mad.

'A Happy Christmas, Bob. A happier Christmas than I have given you for many a year. I'll increase your pay and help your family, and we will talk about these things this afternoon. And now, Bob, make up the fires and buy some more coal before you write another letter.'

The best old man in London

Scrooge did everything he had promised. He did it all and more. He became a good friend and a good master. He was like a second father to Tiny Tim, who did not die, but lived to enjoy many more Christmases. And all in all, old Ebenezer Scrooge became the best old man that good old London knew. Some people laughed at him, but he let them laugh. His own heart laughed, and that was good enough for him.

Scrooge had no more talks with any ghosts, and people said that he knew how to enjoy Christmas better than any other man that lived. If only we can all enjoy our Christmases as well as he did.

And so, in the words of Tiny Tim at the end of that happiest of Christmas Days, 'May God bless us, every one!'

Questions and Activities

1 Scrooge of 'Scrooge and Marley'

Circle the right words or phrases to say what the chapter is about.

1 Ebenezer Scrooge was well known for being very **kind/unkind**.

2 His business was called **E. Scrooge Ltd/Scrooge and Marley**.

3 Jacob Marley **worked in the smaller office/was dead**.

4 The name of Scrooge's **partner/clerk** was Bob Cratchit.

5 'Humbug!' means that Scrooge thought Christmas was **stupid/fun**.

2 The Office is Closed for Christmas

Put these sentences in the right order.

1 Two gentlemen came to Scrooge's office. ☐

2 The kind gentleman said many would rather die than go there. ☐

3 Scrooge would not give them any money, so they went away. ☐

4 They were collecting money for the poor. ☐

5 Scrooge said if they died there would be fewer poor people. ☐

6 Scrooge said there were prisons and poorhouses for poor people. ☐

3 Scrooge Meets an Old Friend

Correct the underlined part of each sentence.

1 Scrooge had his dinner in his office.

2 He amused himself by reading his story book.

3 The door knocker on Scrooge's door turned into a wicked-looking face.

4 As he went up the stairs, he saw a horse.

5 This made him think he was at a wedding.

6 A strange-looking thing came through the wall of Scrooge's room.

4 Scrooge Talks to Marley's Ghost

Put the words in brackets in the right order based on what Marley's ghost said to Scrooge.

1 I made [when] [I was] [this chain] [alive]

I made ______________________________.

2 The chain [about] [comes] [making money] [when] [you think]

The chain ______________________________.

3 You, too, [making] [have been] [for] [a chain] [yourself]

You, too, ______________________________.

4 When I [at the office] [I spent] [was alive] [all my time]

When I ______________________________.

5 I did not [people] [helping] [to think about] [poor] [want]

I did not ______________________________.

6 You [like] [need] [me] [to become] [do not]

You ______________________________.

5 The Ghost of Christmas Past

Which of these descriptions are true, and which are false?

	T	F
1 The Ghost of Christmas Past had the face of a young person.	☐	☐
2 It had long yellow hair.	☐	☐
3 It had a white coat covered with dark green holly leaves.	☐	☐
4 It had a beautiful shining belt.	☐	☐
5 It held some summer flowers in its hand.	☐	☐
6 There was a strange bright light coming from its eyes.	☐	☐

6 Scrooge at Fezziwig's

Who did these things?

Dick	Mrs Fezziwig	young Scrooge
the ghost	old Scrooge	
Mr Fezziwig	the six young men	

1 ______ said, 'It's Christmas. Let's close the office.'

2 ______ brushed the floor, lit the lamps and put coal on the fire.

3 ______ loved the three Miss Fezziwigs.

4 ______ danced alone for a while, after supper.

5 ______ enjoyed everything, and almost laughed at the jokes.

6 ______ said that the people at the party were simple people.

7 ______ said happiness was better than buying something.

7 The Ghost of Christmas Present

Fill in the gaps with the words from the box.

bright	colour	hungry	snow
brushing	fat	meat	snowballs
cooked	good	smell	wrong

The street was not very (1) ______ but it was

full of happy people. There was (2) ________ everywhere. People were (3) ________ it from their paths. Sometimes people threw (4) ________ at each other. If they hit the (5) ________ person, they laughed.

The shop windows were full of light and (6) ________. There were (7) ________ birds hanging in the (8) ________ shops, ready to be taken home and (9) ________.

The (10) ________ of the cakes was so (11) ________ it even made (12) ________ people think they had already eaten too much.

8 Christmas at Bob Cratchit's

Match the beginning of each sentence to the right ending.

1	Mrs Cratchit was dressed •	• **a**	to help him walk.
2	The two smaller Cratchits had smelt •	• **b**	said 'God bless us all'.
3	Bob Cratchit •	• **c**	the wine on the pudding.
4	Tiny Tim used a stick •	• **d**	in bright cheerful colours.
5	Mrs Cratchit set fire to •	• **e**	had been to church with Tiny Tim.
6	Tiny Tim •	• **f**	the goose cooking at the baker's.

9 Christmas at Scrooge's Nephew's House

Put the letters of these words in the right order. The first one has been done for you.

The ghost took Scrooge to the house of Scrooge's
nephew
(1) **wenhep**. Scrooge heard what everyone (2) **othuthg** about him. Scrooge's (3) **eecin** did not like him. But Scrooge's nephew said he thought that his uncle was a (4) **gesrant** old man. He said it was not important that Scrooge was (5) **chir**. Scrooge never did any good with his (6) **enmoy**. He did not even make himself (7) **pyhap** with it.

10 The Ghost of Christmas Yet to Come

Who took these things from the dead man?

the cleaner the laundress the undertaker's man

Bed-curtains ____________
Blankets ____________
Clothes ____________
Jewellery ____________
Sheets ____________
Shoes ____________
Silver buttons ____________
The dead man's best shirt ____________
Towels ____________

11 Tiny Tim is Dead

Fill in the gaps with the words from the box.

better	gravestone	love	shake
cemetery	hope	name	sorry

The ghost took Scrooge to a (1) ________. It pointed to a (2) ________. Scrooge saw his own (3) ________ written there.

Scrooge asked the ghost if there was no (4) ________. The ghost did not answer, but its hand began to (5) ________. Scrooge thought that it was (6) ________ for him.

Scrooge said he would (7) ________ Christmas, and try to think of it all the year. He said that he would be a (8) ________ man.

12 Scrooge Wakes Up on Christmas Morning

The underlined sentences are all in the wrong paragraph. Which paragraph should they go in?

1 The boy outside Scrooge's house told him that it was still Christmas day. <u>Scrooge said he would not allow it any longer.</u> Then he sent it to Bob Cratchit's house in Camden Town. ☐

2 In the street he met the gentleman who had asked for money for the poor. <u>Scrooge said he had come to dinner.</u> The man was very surprised. ☐

3 Scrooge went to his nephew's house. Scrooge said he would give him a lot of money. His nephew was pleased to see him. ☐

4 Bob Cratchit was late coming to work next morning. Scrooge asked him to go and buy a big turkey. Then he increased Bob's pay, and wished him a Happy Christmas. ☐

Book Report

Now write a book report to display in the library or your classroom. These questions will help you.

Title

Type What type of story is your book?

- Adventure
- Classic
- Crime
- Detective story
- Fairy tale
- Horror and suspense
- Mystery
- Play
- Romance
- Science fiction and fantasy
- Short story
- Others

Characters Who are the main characters in the book?

Main characters Describe the main characters.
What do they look like?
What are they like?

Story What is the story about?
Remember not to give the ending away!

My comments What did you think of the story?
Did you enjoy it?
Would you recommend this book to your classmates?

Visit the website and download the book report template
www.oupchina.com.hk/elt/oper

OXFORD PROGRESSIVE ENGLISH READERS

STARTER

The Ant and the Grasshopper and Other Stories by Aesop
Retold by David Foulds

The Brave Little Tailor and Other Stories by the Brothers Grimm
Retold by Katherine Mattock

The Emperor's New Clothes and Other Stories by Hans Christian Andersen
Retold by Janice Tibbetts

Folk Tales from Around the World
Retold by Rosemary Border

Giants, Dragons and Other Magical Creatures
Retold by Philip Popescu

Heroes and Heroines
Retold by Philip Popescu

In the Land of the Gods
Retold by Magnus Norberg

Journey to the West
Retold by Rosemary Border

The Lion and the Mouse and Other Stories by Aesop
Retold by David Foulds

The Little Mermaid and Other Stories by Hans Christian Andersen
Retold by Janice Tibbetts

The Monkey King
Retold by Rosemary Border

Peter Pan
Retold by Katherine Mattock

Level 1

Alice's Adventures in Wonderland
Lewis Carroll

The Call of the Wild and Other Stories
Jack London

Emma
Jane Austen

The Golden Goose and Other Stories
Retold by David Foulds

Jane Eyre
Charlotte Brontë

Just So Stories
Rudyard Kipling

Little Women
Louisa M. Alcott

The Lost Umbrella of Kim Chu
Eleanor Estes

The Secret Garden
Frances Hodgson Burnett

Tales from the Arabian Nights
Edited by David Foulds

Treasure Island
Robert Louis Stevenson

The Wizard of Oz
L. Frank Baum

Level 2

The Adventures of Sherlock Holmes
Sir Arthur Conan Doyle

A Christmas Carol
Charles Dickens

The Dagger with Wings and Other Father Brown Stories
G. K. Chesterton

The Flying Heads and Other Strange Stories
Edited by David Foulds

The Golden Touch and Other Stories
Edited by David Foulds

Gulliver's Travels — A Voyage to Lilliput
Jonathan Swift

The Jungle Book
Rudyard Kipling

Life Without Katy and Other Stories
O. Henry

Lord Jim
Joseph Conrad

A Midsummer Night's Dream and Other Stories from Shakespeare's Plays
Edited by David Foulds

The Mill on the Floss
George Eliot

Nicholas Nickleby
Charles Dickens

Oliver Twist
Charles Dickens

The Prince and the Pauper
Mark Twain

The Stone Junk and Other Stories
D. H. Howe

Stories from Greek Tragedies
Retold by Kieran McGovern

Stories from Shakespeare's Comedies
Retold by Katherine Mattock

Tales of King Arthur
Retold by David Foulds

The Talking Tree and Other Stories
David McRobbie

Through the Looking Glass
Lewis Carroll

Level 3

The Adventures of Huckleberry Finn
Mark Twain

The Adventures of Tom Sawyer
Mark Twain

Around the World in Eighty Days
Jules Verne

The Canterville Ghost and Other Stories
Oscar Wilde

David Copperfield
Charles Dickens

Fog and Other Stories
Bill Lowe

Further Adventures of Sherlock Holmes
Sir Arthur Conan Doyle

Great Expectations
Charles Dickens

Gulliver's Travels — Further Voyages
Jonathan Swift

The Hound of the Baskervilles
Sir Arthur Conan Doyle

The Merchant of Venice and Other Stories from Shakespeare's Plays
Edited by David Foulds

The Missing Scientist
S. F. Stevens

The Pickwick Papers
Charles Dickens

The Red Badge of Courage
Stephen Crane

Robinson Crusoe
Daniel Defoe

Silas Marner
George Eliot

Stories from Shakespeare's Histories
Retold by Katherine Mattock

A Tale of Two Cities
Charles Dickens

Tales of Crime and Detection
Edited by David Foulds

Two Boxes of Gold and Other Stories
Charles Dickens

LEVEL 4

Dr Jekyll and Mr Hyde and Other Stories
Robert Louis Stevenson

Far from the Madding Crowd
Thomas Hardy

From Russia, With Love
Ian Fleming

The Gifts and Other Stories
O. Henry and Others

The Good Earth
Pearl S. Buck

The Great Gatsby
F. Scott Fitzgerald

Journey to the Centre of the Earth
Jules Verne

King Solomon's Mines
H. Rider Haggard

Mansfield Park
Jane Austen

The Moonstone
Wilkie Collins

A Night of Terror and Other Strange Tales
Guy de Maupassant

Othello and Other Stories from Shakespeare's Plays
Edited by David Foulds

The Picture of Dorian Gray
Oscar Wilde

Seven Stories
H. G. Wells

Tales of Mystery and Imagination
Edgar Allan Poe

Tess of the d'Urbervilles
Thomas Hardy

The Thirty-nine Steps
John Buchan

Twenty Thousand Leagues Under the Sea
Jules Verne

The War of the Worlds
H. G. Wells

The Woman in White
Wilkie Collins

You Only Live Twice
Ian Fleming

LEVEL 5

The Diamond as Big as the Ritz and Other Stories
F. Scott Fitzgerald

Dracula
Bram Stoker

Dragon Seed
Pearl S. Buck

Frankenstein
Mary Shelley

Kidnapped
Robert Louis Stevenson

Lorna Doone
R. D. Blackmore

The Mayor of Casterbridge
Thomas Hardy

The Old Wives' Tale
Arnold Bennett

Pride and Prejudice
Jane Austen

The Stalled Ox and Other Stories
Saki

Three Men in a Boat
Jerome K. Jerome

Vanity Fair
William Thackeray

Wuthering Heights
Emily Brontë